The Phoenix Living Poets

OUT ON A LIMB

OUT ON A LIMB

By

MICHAEL BURN

CHATTO AND WINDUS

THE HOGARTH PRESS

1973

Published by
Chatto and Windus Ltd
with The Hogarth Press Ltd
42 William IV Street
London W.C.2

★

Clarke, Irwin & Co. Ltd
Toronto

ISBN 0 7011 1992 6

© Michael Burn, 1973

Printed in Great Britain by
Lewis Reprints Ltd.,
The Brown Knight & Truscott Group
London and Tonbridge

For Mary

Acknowledgements are due to the editors of *Encounter* where several of these poems were first published.

CONTENTS

A DISAPPOINTMENT

Mr. Sulzbacher was disappointed in this author.
I too. We'd been so sure. Sulzbacher ordered
A farm in New Hampshire, and Mrs. Kramp and I
Reserved for a summer in Venice. This author seemed
Possessed, shall I say?, of a sensitivity
Uncommon to-day, a freshness. He lived in the country.
When he came to town he called it 'a huge bazaar,
Like Constantinople'. No one had ever said that;
Or not in our hearing. We saw ourselves on cushions,
Doing something with sherbet. In the outer office
Miss Jackson's eyes turned almond, and all Manhattan
Withdrew behind a yashmak.
We have a superior list, but we were waiting . . .
This *must* be the promised one.

He began with a project about Emily Dickinson.
She was, as he termed it, just making the swing-doors.
The draft had an innocence, a kind of sort of
Adamant tenderness (he named it so himself).
By the time he had finished, Emily Dickinson
Was out on the sidewalk again. His next, an elegy,
Was moving about Grant's Tomb. It took three years.
I won't trouble you with the rest, except to say
He possessed that gift, amounting almost to genius,
Of knowing when the wind of favour would veer,
And of getting his sails up just in the nick of time
To see it veer back again. Everything he composed
Gleamed with that youthfulness very rare in our day.
If we detected sometimes a trace of flatness,
He assured us it was deliberate. He taught us much
About the power of the monosyllable to depress.
Thinking about it, I could not have faced the subway,
Had it not been for the lift of the long U's,
Elided I's and agitation of female endings.
Vowels, he said, were flowers; consonants, railroads
(T's going west, M's east). Punctuation, he said,
Is a poet's Morse. We thought that beautiful.
He was great on assonance. It was great to be taking around

A man in whom you could *sense* the internal rhymes.
We wished only that speech, when it came, fell faster
On to the page. His lines on Paul Valéry in Harlem . . .
There were only two. . .took a year. His first wife
Walked out after his first lyric, and he withdrew it.
We tried to understand, though once he had told us
That a poet's pen is dipped in his tears (a sentiment
Later transferred to rhyme). . . . . . .
                        There were no hard feelings.
He kept to the end that unpolluted quality.
After the advance he never spoke about money.
We did not ask it back, having ourselves been touched
By something of his spiritual deodorant,
If I may put it so, as indeed he put it.

He died while still composing his own epitaph.
Now we no longer take fog-horns for the muezzin.
Miss Jackson's eyes have gone back to blackcurrant.
And by the time we get something from the afterworld,
I fear religious belief will be out again.
In due course a memoir will be in the bookshops,
Though not published by Sulzbacher and Kramp.
He used to say one should not be subject to fashion,
But one has to live. Sulzbacher has no country home.
Mrs. Kramp and I are spending the summer in Brooklyn.

WORDS SENT OUT

Words few will find homes for,
Go out and get lost.
Small words, pointless as humming-birds
In the kestrel sky, go out.
No one will think you worth killing.

Time with its sullenness
The clearest lineaments to vagueness turns,
Her dearest voice will blur,
Splinter the glass, the echo dissipate,
What most seems sure disturb.

Who knows this, will receive you,
Birds of no moment, love-birds,
Fledged by the rainbow years.

ECOLOGY

When the pipeline gasps for oil,
When the ores are down to bone,
No more copper, no more nitrates,
Warmth and light and telephone

More than half-way back to Newton,
Horse and cart and no more coal,
Farmers chopping down the orchards
For a fire to fry a mole;

When the gentlemen and ladies
In that pinched millennium
Riot round the herring trawlers,
Won't another shortage come

In the worn-and-torn to-morrow,
Worse than running-down supplies?
Even she will have grown older;
Even her oasis eyes

Have less strength to sweeten deserts,
Take the tears, and solaced send
Children home, and others older,
Bringing broken hearts to mend.

Earth, what will you do without her?
When the fevers vainly call,
When the heart-ache gets no answer,
When she has no strength at all?

Solar tappings, tidal voltage,
May the oracles of waste disprove;
No laboratory replenish
Such a deficit of love.

NOTHING DOING

Can't you do more. . . . ?
Tell people something will sell,
Who put what where,
How many dames,
How many times,
Grandstand or handstand,
Something more meaty,
Something more fruity,
We could try to get banned?

No, I can't.

Ask Mrs. Nosey Price.
She climbs to our window each night.
Mr. Beau Peep is her lover.
He holds the ladder.
"What's going on?" he says.
"Nothing," she says.
"Writing those verses, and nothing!
Perhaps they're dead?"
"Or probably impotent," she says;
"All that talk!
Poetry . . . . .
People from London too!"
"Mind you don't fall in the flower-bed".

Off to the church-yard, Mrs. Nosey Price.
Olwen and Emrys are trying it twice.
Mr. Beau Peep, come blow up your horn.
The sheep's in the meadow, the meadow's in porn.
Don't forget colour film.
People insist on that.

Have they gone?
Yes.

13

EXEMPTED

She sits in front of her glass,
Leaning her cheek on her hand, a little morose,
And says, "My lines are all going downwards."
She does not know what I know
Of the compact of Time with Beauty . . . . .
To continue his task, the part he cannot evade,
And yet to concede
For this exceptional one, not as a precedent,
Since lines must come, come then as a setting for jewels,
Or faint as the gossamer lines
On a perfectly mended bowl;
Since the body's strength must grow less, then to pass
Into the spirit, the soul,
And to show
In the eyes, that may glitter no more, but shall glow.

So she sits in front of her glass,
Takes off her make-up, ties her hair,
And comes to bed,

Little knowing she has been watching a miracle.

CHILDREN

Not for the statesman's laurels,
Not the heroic palm,
The hopes that once sustained us
When love was slow to warm.
And nearer now, and clearer,
Since hopes too came to harm,

We see, through old misfortune,
Hurt young is hurt for good. . . . . .
My vines won't grow on your hill-side.

My grapes are stained with your blood. . .
These songs at last, my sea-spray,
Flowering on your flood.

So late our light, so different
From lives that find at morn
Contenting plough and pasture,
And home at dark return,
With never a crop not lifted,
And never a lamb not born.

PLEASE!

O God, do something worldly for us!
O, load us with a very large sum of money
Now,
And in any reliable currency
Allow
Us to be surprised. Fill up our dustbin
With packages of undevalued
Yen,
Reichsmark, or the more humbly pursued
Pound.
Begin
Each day with the
Sound
Of a not small cheque.
Let
Paul Get-
-ty and Barbara Hutton take a fancy to either or both of us.
Thrus-
-t several remunerative and gay
Tempta-
-tions in our way,
Such as a
Venice palazzo with a whale-
-scale swimpool, and a
Merc,
Or two Mercs. Arrange for my
Work
To be high-
-ly app-
-lauded everywhere, and re-
-warded beyond its merits. Snap
Thy magnificent fingers, be
Not skimping with largesse,
Tax-free;
For example gold
Francs,
And from untold
Swiss rolls and credits in countless

Banks,
O God, withhold
Not
O not withhold Thy hand.
But
With such mundane meaningless things, Almighty, cover us
    thick
Ageing babes-in-the-wood, and
Cover us quick!

TWO SHORES

Two women who loved one man,
And the man dead,
And the women talking . . . .
Like a sea that shares two shores,
Calm now and warm, coming from great depths,
Waves that make little sound,
And seem hardly to break, telling each shore of the other.

CENSORED

I meet an anonymous
Censor, who
Lets sadism, spite,
And hatred through,

But will not pass,
Or so it seems,
The words Love signs
In our two names.

Then find a chest
To take the best,
And tie them up
With emerald string,

And dig them down
Beneath such tree
As still remains
To you, to me;

And think they share
The formal fate
Omnipotent State
Decrees for men

Accused of some
Too private passion;
Where out of fashion
Is hors de la loi;

Singers unknown
From light cut off;
And so our own
Small witness add,

In this free country,
If ever found,
Here too the heart
Went underground.

HERS AND MINE

If you could wear words,
These might do the trick.
You could come to a grand evening party,
Dressed head to toe in poetry.

The Empress of the Turds,
The President of the Twenty-Fourth Republic,
Herr Mustikoff and the Mormon Ambassador would murmur,
"Who is that charmer?".

Mounseer Trousseau (et Cie.
Turnover millions of gold francs annually)
Would ask the way to your couturier,
And crab-like hands

Grab down through arc-lamps at your sleeves, your train.

In vain.
And Mounseer ask in vain.
There is no blue-print for the trade
Of you, or what are yours, yours only, and
I made.

TILL DOOMSDAY

When in my cleverness
I smothered her,
She rose up from the bed,
And put my clothes away.
When in my bitterness
I stabbed her,
She washed away the blood,
And made our bedroom gay.
When in my sullenness
I drowned her,
She walked home by the sands,
And did things needed doing.

Only her eyes showed bruising.
The sea was in her hands,
And loneliness the wound.
She kept a diary that will not be found.
To the world, the perfect pair. I've never written
The story of those murders. There has been
No trial, all being frustrate; even
My own upon myself she thwarted. She
Encouraged me to express
My thoughts' excesses more romantically. . . .

Hiker or antiquary,
Dragging the ivy from our century,
Know our worn monument
Tells of the world one Irish heart the less,
The gayest Ireland ever sent
To dance on English ground;
And with her me,
By her got ready for eternity.
And any thrush that's heard
In storm or snow, or other quiet bird,
Sings as executor of my will,
And shall, until
My debt is quit

For love she gave,
And gives,
Till doomsday sound.

WHAT I SEE

Vienna, yellow and green.
London, lavender.
Steel, for New York.
Pekin, a jewelled bird.
Urbino, white; Rome, golden.
Venice, a treasure raised.

And on these hills, this estuary,
Despair of painters, faithless,
Still difference in one place,
Still smiles, still sulks, still change,
A mood for every minute.
Stay for a picture, Wales!

Be something always!
Home of the looking-for-home.
Light like a pole-vaulter
Skims summits, and is gone.
The diamond windows darken.
The raven clouds sail on.

A LAKE

I've often dreamed that someone else
Will one day feel the way I've felt,
And say so, after I am dead,
In words or phrases I once made:
And now and then I've tried to guess
Which words they'd be, and what the cause.

They might be from the lathe where love
Has toiled through nights I should have saved,
Or rags my scarecrow mind has used
To frighten off unwelcome news,
Or some of those malign grotesques
Turned up at nobody's request.
But when at last the moment came,
It had not been in any dream.

In a green collar-bone of hills,
A stone's-throw from the sky, in Wales,
We came upon a little tarn,
So sky-reflecting, taciturn,
So white, expectant, and enchanted—
An air-strip for a magic carpet—
It seemed that all the western myths
Had risen from its peaty depths.
Three boat-lengths thick all round the shore
The water-lilies were in flower,

And king-cups thrust their yellow heads
Between the blue glass of the reeds.
And looking at that lake I felt
A century or two annulled.
Exactly as I was that day——
Those lilies lying in the sky,
That stillness, and that secrecy!—
So other men one day would be.
The longing tugging at my heart
Had tugged at people in the past,
And would at many unborn people:
To utter thanks, and be unable.

TURNING OFF

Bumper to bumper. Four miles from coast to church.
Constable Griffiths cut that snake in two
To admit a family in a family car.
Hoping to travel faster a longer way,
They had turned off yesterday on minor roads,
And become hysterical.

They had seen things.

They had met at twilight a defeated cortège,
Guarding a dying king in a tattered litter
To a shore where three queens waited.
When dark fell,
A winged horse leapt from the mountains
And left, wherever he touched, horseshoes of lights
That disappeared in a lake. At midnight
A sword waved from the lake's blackness, and seven swans
Sailed past, wearing coronets.
A courier bent low and shouted something.
The air was torn with cries.
In the small hours' silence
They had heard the rocks pushing, the slow shoving
In earth's night, the slip, the slide, and the inrush
Of oceans, and wind slicing the summits;
And had seen the crystals that glittered as they formed
Round the dead gossiping in crevices five hundred
Million years before Christ, and an old lady
In her winding-sheet, muttering as in life;
While those for whom the willow weeps in slate
Whistled in the deep dark veins
Under the chert and quartz.
Dawn had brought ghosts of the sea
Streaming along the saltings, then farm after farm
Took off like seagulls into a thunder sky.
But when sun rose
Apples were golden in cottage gardens
And fleeces touched with gold.

"You saw all that?"
"Yes. . . .yes!"
"O, but we never bother with it".
So, some inhabitants; or else,
"We seldom see it now".

The strangers are reassured.
It had seemed so clear something was about to be born.
But unprepared
By any hint in the weather report or guide-book
This turning-off had made them at first uneasy,
Then afraid, then so nearly mad,
They felt it a kind of bliss to be reincorporated
Into the snake again, embedded fore and aft
In the familiar nuisances.

You could have seen them later
Picnicking a couple of yards from the road,
Perfectly self-possessed.

A WITCH MISSING

One witch when I was baptised
Failed to make it.
Too busy for me, I take it,
Whirling around on her motorised

Besom, she missed my chimney.
On others she showered
A gift she wasn't empowered,
Didn't want, or forgot, to give me.

Hopelessly out of the swim
Through her neglect,
At cup-finals of intellect
There's always a favourite team,

Whose colours I can't wear;
A dominant sound
Swells up from all sides of the ground
Somehow I can't manage to share.

Despair's what that peregrine hag
Gave to many, but not
To me; and it nags me a lot,
Shorting on that one plug. . .

That porridge my spirit's diet
Seems to have missed,
And no psychiatrist
So far has known how to supply it.

People say everything's lost.
I can't get it,
Or regret I can't get it.
What's this truth that's been pinched from my post?

What *is* it, wrong with my timing?
Out on a limb,
Impossible Sunny Jim
Or perambulant silver lining.

Perhaps she'll turn up at the end;
Say, "Here, I forgot.
Think you're lucky?   You're not.
O-ho, mustn't grumble, my friend?

Just wait!" But by then, touch wood,
I'll be too far gone,
Beyond disillusion,
I'll be blind in one eye for good.

COMMON SENSE

i

In the imperium of common sense
(In a country close, a not far from present tense?)
Books of the rules all read, they have room to see
Through an ephemeral wood an immortal tree.

O so much written, and so much learnt!
Cries, confessions, and ashes of men burnt,
So many stakes and scaffolds, so many scrawls
Decoded from the blood on prison walls!

Russia lay down without anaesthetic
For a fifty-year operation, a public physic.
Where the authentic cure, where the pretence,
Why it went wrong, all know, and the instruments.

Time then to pickaxe that disastrous play,
Dustbin that skein of the past, the soggy overspun
Tangle of have and have-not, of we and they,
Sad and ridiculous as the mastodon!

In the imperium of common sense
They have got off the gibbets at last and taken wing,
And pensioned the Furies with their boring knitting.
Love is their law, reason is their defence.

So blinding this view, I almost heard again
The shepherds stumbling homeward, and the heavens tell
Traditional joy, and out of the sunset swell
Bells of Atlantis under the main.

Where, where this place?   About that, silence;
Though nearer perhaps than we think. I am only aware,
Others might not, but I should like to live there,
In the imperium of common sense.

ii

With the same tenderness
As lovers climb the stair;
With the same grace, same dash,
As divers make
Their arrow in the air
A perfect somersault, arrow again, and break
The water with hardly a splash;
With the same confidence, delight,
As airmen try
Their ski-turns in the blue, their blue and white
Picassos in the sky. . . . .

Will no one come
Out on some balcony and say,
It's all so beautiful, so clear. . . .
Neither a hero nor a saviour. . .
No somebody appear,
Servant of no such grand conception
As of Redemption, History, or Will,
But purely to fulfil
The same responsive human love for living,
As love for love, for flying, or for diving?

FANATICS

This razor-edge is classed as Most Severe.
Nobody not a little mad attempts it.
Hands freeze on holds.   No precipice abates
The excitement of their certainty and fear.

For this they know is Life, to grapple fiends
That shriek in the snow's whirled nebulae, see God
In spasms of sheer thrill, but mostly plod
Sullenly towards a summit that is not there.

Such is Infatuation.   Single of body or mind,
Its athletes cannot quit that storm-black ridge,
Thinking they see, not knowing they are blind,
Contemptuous of the sun on either side.

ENGLAND AND ELSEWHERE

Here what are tensions
There become truncheons.

There death is worn outside;
Here, under all wears, hides.

Here it's a tricky vote;
There it's the tongue torn out.

Here who in prison sigh
There are pegged out to die.

Tiger and shark preside
There; here on leashes ride.

There the hyenas flourish;
Here there's no cage for courage.

There with a belted guard;
Here in a mental ward.

Here what they drink is fizz;
There it was jailer's piss.

Here it is chips and steak;
There their own shit they ate.

Here it's retired or fired;
There it's your balls they've wired.

Here it is Ayes and Noes;
There it is shrieks and blows.

Here it's a damned disgrace;
There just another case.

Here it's Old Nick controlled;
There it's the nightmare throned. . . .

So I've believed it to be.
Still in cold sweat I see
There the crowned eyes of fear
Here through bland visors peer;
Here in a club armchair,
Here at a table bare,
Jobless or millionaire,
Sadist with moron's stare,
Or all the ages' heir,
Cheating the nurses' care,
Waiting with smarmed-down hair,
Debating with snow-white hair,
Dreaming of guns to wear,
Beatings, and flesh to tear,
Waiting with time to spare,
Aching to see what's there,
Aching to be what's there.

ON A SPY

This is the grave of a most dedicated
Someone, to whom we opened homes and beds,
And gave the latch-key to our hearts,
The spare-room in our heads;

Whom we could never bore, who always loved us
Purely, devotedly, to give away,
And single-mindedly pursued us
In hope of bigger quarries to betray.

Such patience, opening other people's letters;
Such plodding-on, in so obscure a trade;
So much fidelity to wife and friends;
Such long hours fooling them!   And all unpaid.

SAMSON AGONISTES:
A Philistine Speaks to the Children of Israel

There came that terrible roar.
And then the huge hot breath.
The house bulged, it seemed a colossal whale
Was sucking it in. . . .then screams.
I can't talk about the rest.

Go and interview someone else.
No, stop.   I'll ask you something.
Were we all that wicked,
All of us, one and all,
All deserved to be crushed, mutilated, the sights you've seen. . .?
You've watched them getting the bodies out.

I didn't feel well that day.
That's why I didn't go.
And now you come with your hymns and collecting-boxes,
Asking my personal impressions. . .
"Don't you think it proves we were right?
Our God's won, won't you join us?"
Just leave me alone.
Leave me here in my empty house.
Leave me to go to the office,
Passing our temple's ruins each morning and evening,
With my wife and kids still buried under the rubble.
"Come, come, no time for lamentation now. . ."!
Don't dare name Samson here.

Don't speak to me.

EPITAPH ON THE DIPHTHONG

Shapes of grammar, spelling, accents,
Symbols of inconstancy!
Only one appeared to be
Keeping ancient permanence.

Hyphenated words divorce,
Live alone, or form liaisons
With seven others all at once.
Not a word respects its source.

Words mutate and make fresh starts.
In official paragraphs
Pauses rare as the giraffe.
Brackets always lived apart,

Like inverted commas, who
May be doubles. Rows of dots
Offer vagueness, where full-stops,
Though more truthful, might not do.

Back to Rome or on to hippy—
Hono(u)r, favo(u)r, drop-out U.
Socks are sox, and through is thru.
Won(')t without apostrophe.

Anarchy in punctuation:
Semi-colon, stylist's pride,
Broken up and thrown aside;
Colon, just an affectation.

Till a little while ago
In the diphthong you might find
Letters changelessly entwined,
A and E, and E and O.

Nothing, so it seemed, could move
Double vowels so commingled
As inseparable singles,
Spelling's symbol of true love.

"Vulgar usage," scholars state.
Now the diphthong's seen no more.
Spelling must obey the law:
Two are always separate.

Something I should like to know:
When the alphabet was rid
Of the diphthong's love-knot, did
What was symbolised go too?

KILLED IN ULSTER

In memory of Sergeant Malcolm Banks, 29, British soldier, who had started a scheme to help handicapped children in Belfast, and was killed a few minutes before the ceasefire of June 1972.

The man she had lost
Softly slid the latch one night,
Sat down in firelight;
Just as he had been
On his last leave.

Played with the children.
Asked after neighbours.
Took her away,
Gave the awaited holiday,
In a country where death

Could not take off,
Nor sniper spit nor mortar cough.
By a stream not poisoned
They talked of children,
Those he had helped

In the bitter war,
Laughing and serious
By the broken water,
While the dappled day went by.
In a stranger's eye

There they are always,
Heads close and arms
Round each other's shoulders laid,
Mingled for ever,
Sunlight and shade.

HATING SOMETHING

Heron.
Hieratic, frigid, stiff.
Like an Inquisitor,
Or one of those thin Egyptians,
Who learned how stars wheeled or Nile flooded,
And claimed to prophesy;
Or like a speculator,
Never missing the tide,
Hunched by rivers,
Pinching the water's edge,
Snipping the flood like a market. . .
Down, down like dollars
That lean mean throat
Go dabs and sea-trout,
Fish swimming in trustingly from the sea-caves,
Scudding and silver fish.

It is also ridiculous.
A flying giraffe with rickets;
Beak as thin as its legs,
Wings like a mad inventor's,
That you think can't work; when it banks,
One will come off . . .but it doesn't.
Heron, birds' attorney,
Official Receiver of birds,
Wings stuffed thick with deeds,
Rimless specs on its beak,
Patron-bird of police-States,
Prayed to by spies.

And grey, grey with a bit of white,
As if rain stood up.
Its only dream to swallow the rainbow.

O well, it's something
Only to hate the heron.

Think of a heron in love!

FOR THE COMMON MARKET

It's easy to be witty in French.
You don't have to know French well.
Think of those French expressions (this is the secret) . . .
Goût du néant, esprit de l'escalier,
Dégoût de la vie, nostalgie de la boue,
Adieu suprême des mouchoirs.
All you have to do is take two nouns,
Any old nouns, the iller-assorted the better,
And couple them with a genitive,
Shrug, throw your hands out (not too far),
In a French sort of way,
And give the casual knowing look of someone
Who knows the girl at the bar.
Try it and see. . .
With faint disdain. . .c'est un sentiment de vestiaire,
Amour de boulanger, fantaisie du lavabo,
Goût de Londres, tendresse des wagons-lits,
Or sighing
Les aurevoirs de Vendredi.
Everyone will say how well you know French.
I've tried it on Frenchmen, and I know.

In German just couple the words together,
Like any old strangers meeting in any old street. . .
Himmelschnabel Apfelpudel Heldenbegeisterung Weltkrebs. . .
No one will know any better.

In Italian it will be helpful to know the first line of Dante,
And also, brushing away a tear,
Italia, Italia, terra di morti,
And go straight on to business.

I will advise later about the Scandinavian countries.

FOR MOURA BUDBERG
On her proposed departure from England

Yes, age deserves
Some quiet, as had youth——
Or so you've told us.
Is that the truth?
Isn't it a fact
That Talleyrand adored you,
And for your want of tact
In the Commune of eighteen-seventy
Marx praised and Eugénie deplored you?

Old ships look home
To harbours they once knew.
Had you such harbours?
Honestly, weren't you
There at Pompeii,
Saved out of the lava
By your great love-to-be?
Did you have words with Madame Bovary?
And weren't you Tolstoy's girl at Balaclava?

Brilliant balloons
Of fantasy and gossip
Inflate to legends,
Till we make up
Twenty, not one,
Swans to whom you were Leda.
How well *did* you know Solomon?
And was he wise?   In Berlin, certainly,
The Kaiser took you for the Queen of Sheba.

That you were born
Is also sure, and bred
In deepish purple.
You preferred red.
Grey's not your wear,
London not yours to nest in,
Not now, not any more.
Too many rats.   Where to then, citizen-
Baroness, what fresh fields to rest in?

What country to appease
So hungry a delight
In one friend, or many,
Tracing all night
To some old thought
Contemporary ferment;
The Revolution, or the Court;
Talking your casual documentary,
Where every scene seems happening that moment?

Well, join your son.
Give the last party,
And vanish, placing
In the last taxi
Their books men signed,
The letters in the folders,
London's mists left behind,
Your massive shadow fitly lengthening
Not on a grey wall but a golden.

Let it be Italy.
There you'll have snow,
And there'll be moujiks,
Bells, like Moscow,
And just as before
A family to love you,
And riots, and the poor,
And days to dream of the victorious
Sunflower of Russia who once blazed above you.

GHOST

"Anyone who believes that needs his head looking at.
Eyewash," he said,
Declamatory ex cathedra in front of the grate,
With legs spread

As if to the public, but really to no one more
Than a faded wife,
Who, as he passes in corridors of the expensive raw
Tomb he calls life,

Seems always to shrink aside into the walls,
Living in fear
To be caught with a friend he wouldn't approve, or phone-call
He mustn't hear.

And as one accustomed to being fattened and fed
By her pale attentions,
"I've never seen any ghost in this house," he repeated.
"Ghosts are inventions".

THREE ALONE

One night she came home unexpectedly.
He acted fast asleep. He saw her stare
At him for a long time, then at the book

Where he'd been reading of a distant country.
As usual, she chain-smoked. She seemed unsure
Whether to kiss him, or say something; then went out.

It was a dream, of course. He'd locked the door.
His hair stands up, as if he saw this morning
The night-light, and the saucer, and the stubs.

His father smoked a pipe. They seldom spoke.
They were the only people living there.
And he was twelve then, much too young to smoke.

ABDICATION   December 1936 — June 1972

And if Hamlet had come to the throne?

"Extra! Extra!"
The new King announces:
Victory Square to be re-named after his father;
Ophelia to be buried in holy ground
(The Archbishop agrees);
An amnesty, for all involved in the recent troubles:
A Constitution, modelled on England;
Horatio President of the Council;
Royal Visit to Unemployed.
"Something Must Be Done," says King.
"Elsinore liberated . . a new broom," report the Ambassadors.
Where ghosts stalked, fireworks.

How many times, since and before,
The new broom?   Imaginations that create
From their own staleness a new-born nation;
Acclaim of poets in need of enthusiasm;
Apoplexy of war-heroes, retired honourably
To hunting-lodges in the Lapland forests;
Foreign fashions at Court, the divorcées
Peacocking on the great stairs.

The growlings of the charcoal-burners
Will, by the presence at their
Annual Gala, of the King himself,
Be somewhat satisfied. News also comes of
Subsidies to the whale-fisheries; this will appease
The truculent North.   And for the first time the
Budget is balanced. Many reductions are promised
In the price of essential foods.

And after a while
The country learns of a rival in Hamlet's heart.
Rumours sieved through the palace
Rain on the counting-houses,
Reaching the cottages last.
Goings-on, tales of extravagance;

The old Queen's ruby
Ablaze like Sirius between alien breasts;
The woodcutter is blinded by millions of candles,
Melting the midnight snow encircling pavilions
A plumed élite patrol;
And the startled reindeer run South with alarming stories
Of moonlight sleigh-rides, a royal love run wild
Over a laughing face half-hidden in sables.

Bishops are being appointed
For their looks and youth alone;
Schools left half-built for caskets from Paris;
A hospital sacrificed to pay for a banquet
For a new ally (Horatio side-stepped),
Whom the Council have not approved. Demonstrations,
About rising prices. Arrests.
The Constitution withdrawn.
Appeals,
Petitions,
Answered with masques and fêtes.

Till it ends as it ended before.
"Extra! Extra!
Horatio Resigns!"
Fortinbras has been summoned
To restore the old values, establish discipline,
Expel the musicians, supply confidence to the Army.

It will have given the people something to talk about,
A scandal more interesting than the price of meat,
In which a reduction is promised.
The veteran Marshal
Resumes his sword, shakes out a mothy pelisse,
And offers his services to the new dynasty.
And on the frontier
A coach with the blinds drawn down
And a few horsemen are crossing to a farewell salvo
For a promising Prince, a brilliant spinner of words.

Sad, sad, it was only words.

A LAST MENTION

Places I haven't written about,
A mention now.   Forgive
That no rhyme came,
Though not for want of thought,
For you especially,
Quarry, gashed, gaunt,
Silver against black mountains,
Or black against white cloud, where daily I've
Imagined names of the immortals carved;
Beeches and sycamores, so brilliant-green,
With shadows between, raven as Welshmen's hair;
Small birds, feeding in such fear
They must get ulcers; owl,
Hooting whenever a plank of light from the door
Falls by his tree; absolving
Waters, between whom and hills
Dangles this Ithaca of ours; and every
Till now protector, how or wheresoever,
Or riding on or rising from the sea, or
Wind-blown from past knowing; all
Who came, will come, us here, us one day gone;
Farms, meadows, roses;
A people garrulous, withdrawn,
And quiet as the house,
As this page closes.